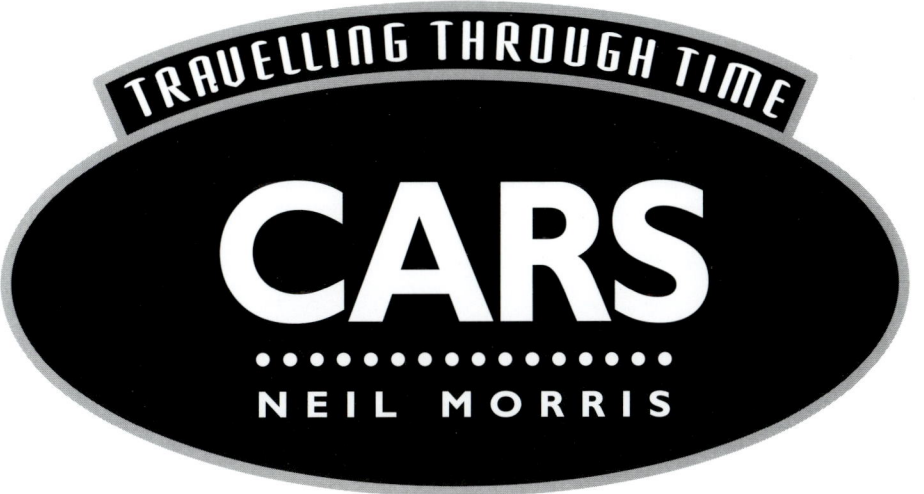

TRAVELLING THROUGH TIME

CARS

NEIL MORRIS

Belitha Press

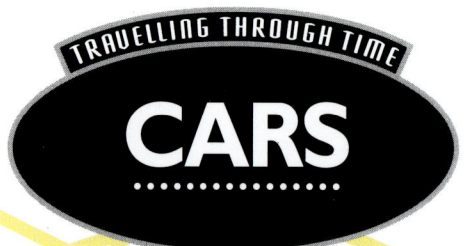

TRAVELLING THROUGH TIME

CARS

First published in the UK in 1997 by
Belitha Press Limited,
London House, Great Eastern Wharf,
Parkgate Road, London SW11 4NQ

ISBN 1 85561 583 5

British Library Cataloguing in Publication Data
for this book is available from the British Library

Printed in Hong Kong

Editor: Jinny Johnson
Designer: Guy Callaby
Picture researcher: Juliet Duff

Words in **bold** appear in the glossary on pages 30–31

Picture acknowledgements:
t=top; b=bottom; c=centre; r=right

Allsport: 24t, 25.
Chrysler Jeep: 28b.
E.T. Archive: 8t.
Mary Evans Picture Library: 12 (both).
Robert Harding Picture Library: 21t.
Hulton Getty Picture Collection: 5t, 13b.
Ludvigsen Associates: 8–9b.
The National Motor Museum, Beaulieu: 13t, 17 (both).
Photri Inc: 4–5b.
Quadrant Picture Library: 9t, 16b, 20c, 29b.
Retrograph Archive Ltd: 16t.
Science Photo Library: 29c.
Topham Picturepoint: 20t.
TRH Pictures: 20–21b.
Vauxhall Motors Ltd: 28t, 29t.
Volkswagen: 5b.

Front cover and main artworks by Terry Hadler
All other artworks by Graham Rosewarne

Contents

Introduction

Cars were first driven along by petrol engines towards the end of the nineteenth century. Since then, they have had an enormous influence on people's lives. The car was not invented by one single person: many inventors and engineers played a part in its development. In the early days, engineers were most interested in the machine that makes the car go – the engine. Later car-makers thought more about the vehicle itself and what it would be like to drive.

▲ Driving through Hyde Park, London in 1922.

◄ Lane after lane of slow-moving traffic – a common scene all over the world.

▼ This new Beetle will try and repeat the success of the 'people's car' first built in the 1930s.

the new Beetle

Rapid growth

Although the first cars were driven by steam, most of the successful cars of the twentieth century have been powered by the **internal-combustion engine**, which burns fuel. This type of engine was first built in 1860 by the French engineer Jean Joseph Étienne Lenoir, using coal gas as fuel. The internal-combustion engine was soon adapted to run on **petrol**, and the number of cars rapidly increased. At first these new vehicles were owned by rich people, but their popularity grew when mass production made them more affordable.

The car takes over

In the last 50 years, the car has completely taken over for short private journeys. As more and more people were able to afford cars, they relied less on other forms of transport such as railways. Bigger, faster roads were built, which made travelling easier for larger road vehicles. Buses and coaches now provide a passenger service between cities, and lorries compete with goods trains for carrying cargo. This has brought even more traffic on to the roads, often causing jams and polluting the air with **exhaust fumes**.

Changing times

People are looking at new ways of using the motor car, to the benefit of everyone. Many cities have become clogged with vehicles, so car-free **pedestrian zones** are now common. Car-makers have found ways to reduce **pollution**, and new forms of energy are being looked at, such as electric cars. Road safety is also an issue. Cars and roads need to be designed with safety in mind, so that fewer people are killed and injured in road accidents. The pioneers of the motor car 100 years ago did not have to think about such things. They had no idea that by the 1990s manufacturers would be producing 35 million new cars every year.

5

The first cars

People first travelled in petrol-driven cars at the
end of the last century. But inventors had
dreamed of building a 'horseless carriage' for
a long time before that. Most of the
early machines were driven by
steam, like railway locomotives
without the rails!

Karl Benz launched his first four-wheeler, the *Viktoria*, in
Germany in 1893. It was not an overnight success, and only
45 cars were sold in the model's first year of production.
The car had an upright steering handle and solid tyres and
did not give an easy or comfortable ride.

Steam carriages

A French engineer named Nicolas Cugnot built a three-wheeled steam tractor in 1769. Just over 30 years later in England, Richard Trevithick designed a steam-driven four-wheeler that carried passengers. But these early steamers were not popular. Many travellers preferred the faithful horse and carriage, and stagecoach companies did not like the competition. Trevithick went on to build the world's first steam locomotive, and railway trains were running in Britain by 1825. At the same time, engineers were working on engines that ran on coal gas, electricity and eventually petrol.

German engineering

Three German engineers were separate founders of the motor car. In 1876, Nikolaus Otto built the forerunner of today's car engine, though his early version ran on coal gas. Then, in 1885, Karl Benz built a three-wheeler powered by an engine that ran on benzine, a form of petrol which could be bought in chemists' shops. This very simple vehicle was the first car to go on sale to the public, and eight years later Benz was selling his four-wheeler. A third German engineer, Gottlieb Daimler, worked originally with Otto. Daimler developed his own petrol engine, and in 1895 he too started building cars. The motoring age had begun.

Around the world

The new technology spread rapidly. In France, Émile Levassor produced a new type of **chassis**, or frame, to fit a Daimler engine. His Panhard-Levassor car of 1891 was the first to have the engine at the front, and this design was soon taken up by others. In the United States, the Duryea brothers built their first car in 1893, and three years later their company sold 13 automobiles! Early British cars were based on Daimler engines, until the first cars built by English engineer Frederick Lanchester went into production in 1901.

◄ Karl Benz (1844–1929), carefully watching the road ahead and using the steering handle to drive his three-wheeler in 1886. Benz took out a **patent** on this first petrol-driven car in the same year. It had a very simple engine, with one gear, which drove the rear wheels by means of chains, like a bicycle. Its top speed was 12 kilometres per hour. Early sales were not good. In 1888 Benz's wife, Bertha, took her two sons for a drive of almost 100 kilometres, to show how reliable the car was. But it was some years before the motoring craze caught on.

► The very first Mercedes car, which was launched in 1901. Most motoring experts call this the first modern motor car. It was designed by Wilhelm Maybach, a partner in Gottlieb Daimler's engineering firm. The car was named after Mercedes Jellinek, the daughter of the Austro-Hungarian Consul in Nice. Emil Jellinek bought and raced Daimler cars, and he encouraged Maybach to build this sporty new model. It had four **gears**, with a very fast top speed of 80 kilometres per hour, and it won the Nice road race in its first year.

LEADING WITH A FLAG

Steam-car and later petrol-car development was held back in Britain by a law introduced in 1865. This stated that all 'road locomotives' had to have two drivers and a person walking ahead of the vehicle with a red flag to warn of its approach. The speed limit of 3 kilometres per hour kept cars in pace with their flag-man. When the law was changed in 1896, the red flag was dropped and the speed limit went up to 23 kilometres per hour.

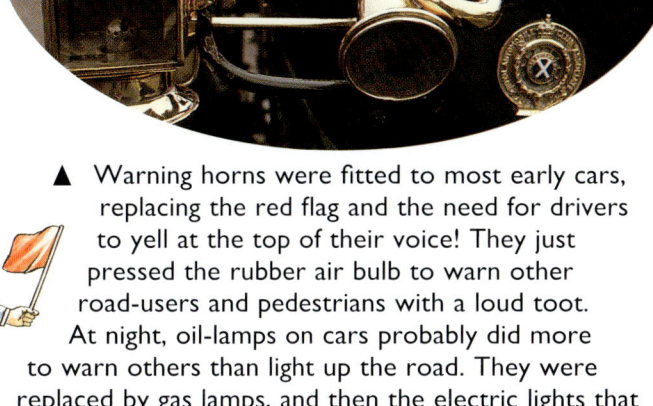

▲ Warning horns were fitted to most early cars, replacing the red flag and the need for drivers to yell at the top of their voice! They just pressed the rubber air bulb to warn other road-users and pedestrians with a loud toot. At night, oil-lamps on cars probably did more to warn others than light up the road. They were replaced by gas lamps, and then the electric lights that are still used today. Most of these items were made of brass. This meant that car-owners, or their servants, had a lot of cleaning and shining to do to keep their prized possession looking smart.

9

Mass production

During the first 20 years of the motor car, each model was individually designed by an engineer. Most cars were separately built by craftsmen, so they took a long time to produce and were very expensive. But the growing American motor industry soon changed all that.

The Model T Ford was nicknamed 'Tin Lizzie'. It was 3.4 metres long and had a top speed of 64 kilometres per hour. Like all cars at that time, early models were started by turning a **crank handle** under the **radiator**. This had to be done carefully to avoid a sprained wrist!

Changing conditions

At the end of the nineteenth century, motoring was catching on in Europe and the United States. But at that time it was an uncomfortable pastime. Driver and passengers generally rode in open vehicles, exposed to the wind and rain. And when it was dry, the unmade roads threw up clouds of dust. Cars were also very expensive, both to buy and to keep running well. Most people couldn't afford them, and by 1900 there were only 8000 cars in the whole of the United States.

New methods

In 1901 the Olds Company produced 425 cars in its Detroit factory. Two years later, Henry Ford formed the Ford Motor Company, and in 1908 he launched a car that was to change the US motor industry. It was the Model T, which sold more than 10 000 in its first year. As sales rose over the next few years, Ford managed to cut the car's price. Then in 1913 he introduced a moving assembly line into his factory. As the cars were pulled along the line, each worker quickly added just one part. Instead of taking days or even weeks to make a complete car, Ford's workers could produce one in an hour and a half.

Success story

In 1916 the Ford factory produced more than half a million Model Ts, and by 1924 this number had risen to two million. At the same time, Ford's mass-production methods meant that the price of a Model T had dropped below $300, a third of its original price 16 years earlier. Model Ts were soon being made in factories in England, Germany and France. It has been calculated that in the early 1920s half the cars in the world were Tin Lizzies!

► This 1920s Ford assembly line shows clearly how Henry Ford's new manufacturing system worked. At each stage of the moving line, a worker or pair of workers is fitting a single part to the chassis. Different body styles were added later in another part of the factory.

The introduction of the assembly line meant that the workers produced more cars for the same wages. Mass production made cars cheaper, which in turn meant that more were sold.

12

◄ Henry Ford (1863-1947) looks proud as he sits in a Model T with his son, Edsel. Production of the Model T in America came to an end in 1927, when Henry Ford drove the 15 millionth Tin Lizzie off the production line in Detroit. Assembly went on around the world for some time after that, and altogether more than 16 million Model Ts were made.

DRIVING A MODEL T

*The driver increased speed by moving the **throttle** control on the steering wheel with his hand. There were two forward gears. When the left foot-pedal was pressed down, the car was in first gear. When it was released, the car went into second gear. You pressed the middle pedal to reverse. The right pedal operated the brakes, and the hand brake could also be used in an emergency. The only **dashboard** instrument was an ammeter, which measured the electric current.*

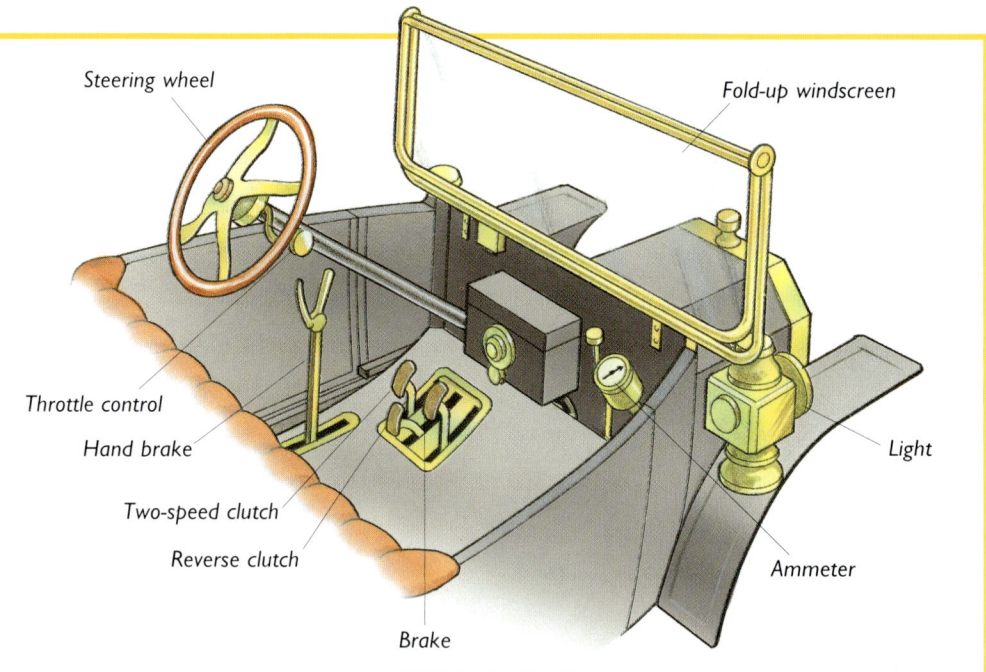

Steering wheel

Fold-up windscreen

Throttle control

Hand brake

Two-speed clutch

Reverse clutch

Light

Ammeter

Brake

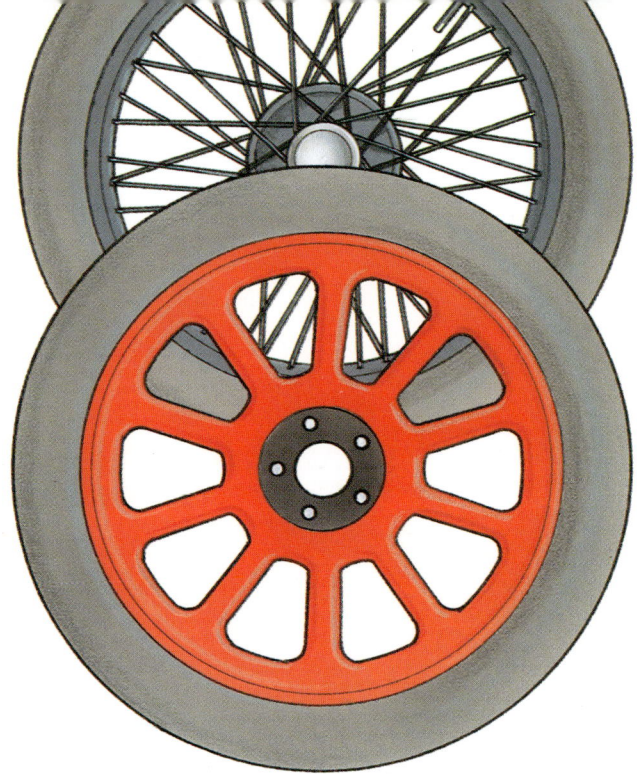

▼ The little Renault AX first took to French roads in 1908. Louis Renault (1877-1944) was the first car manufacturer to replace bicycle-type chains with a shaft to drive the rear wheels. Another advantage of the three-speed AX was that the radiator, which cooled the engine, was mounted just in front of the dashboard. This helped to heat the inside of the car in winter, making motoring much more pleasant.

▲ The first tyres were made of solid rubber. Air-filled tyres were first put on French cars in 1895 by the Michelin brothers. Early tyres were on wooden wheel-rims. By 1910 these had been replaced by steel wheels (above), which could be taken off and replaced by a spare wheel in minutes. This was important at a time when punctures were common because of the poor roads.

Wire spokes (above, top) were introduced in the 1920s. They were light and strong, and were used for many years on fast sports cars.

► Heavy traffic at Piccadilly Circus, London in 1912. The roads are full of cars, horse-drawn carts, double-decker buses and pedestrians. Policemen did their best to direct traffic, but it is easy to see why more controls were needed as the motor car became more popular. No road signs can be seen.

Today, Piccadilly Circus is a mass of traffic lights, signs and pedestrian crossings. Open-topped buses are still used, but only for sight-seeing.

Two years after this picture was taken, the First World War started. To encourage petrol saving, signs went up in London saying 'Don't use a motor car for pleasure'!

Motoring in luxury

Henry Ford built cars that many ordinary working people could afford. But there was always a demand, as there still is today, for motoring luxury. During Ford's time and later, some of the smaller car manufacturers ignored mass production and concentrated on comfort and style.

The Rolls-Royce Phantom II was launched in 1930. Its engine produced six times as much power as the Tin Lizzie, and it could speed along at up to 145 kilometres per hour. In those days Rolls-Royce did not make the **coachwork**, or body, of their cars. This was done to order by expert coachbuilders.

The Ghost and the Phantom

English engineer Henry Royce was not happy with the cars he could buy in the early 1900s, so he decided to build his own. In 1904 he met Charles Stewart Rolls, who sold cars and was very impressed with the Royce model. The two men went into partnership, and Rolls-Royce was born. In 1907 the new company built the famous Silver Ghost, which many called the best car in the world because of its supreme quality. Three years later, Rolls was killed in a plane crash. Royce carried on, also designing aircraft engines, and in 1925 Rolls-Royce launched their first Phantom model.

Chauffeur-driven quality

Phantoms I and II, as well as later models, kept up the Rolls-Royce tradition of quality. Today, the name Rolls-Royce is often used by people to refer to anything which is the very best of its kind. Most of the 1930s models were driven by specially trained, uniformed chauffeurs, who sometimes called themselves 'driver-mechanics', for they did much more than simply drive their employers. It was the chauffeur's job to look after the car, keeping it clean and working perfectly. Rich people usually had more than one car, as they do today, so that they could have the right coachwork for every occasion.

Traffic builds up

In the 1930s, as rich people were driven about in their luxury cars and the less rich drove themselves in their smaller vehicles, roads began to get congested. People living in big cities such as London and New York had to get used to traffic jams and rush-hours. Traffic was still often directed by policemen giving hand signals. Traffic lights had been introduced in the 1920s, and now they started to spread rapidly. Imagine the chaos and danger in cities without them!

15

◄ Bugatti was one of the most famous makes of luxury cars and racing cars of the 1930s. The huge Bugatti Royale was 6.7 metres long, and only six were built. In 1990 the Royale became the most expensive car ever, when one was sold privately for $15 million.

► By the time of the 1929 Paris motor show there were many different makes of car. Since then some of the smaller companies have closed down, while others have joined together to form the huge corporations that exist today.

Car companies have always used the world's motor shows to launch their new models to the press and the general public. The year 1929 saw exciting new models of the American Chevrolet, German Opel and French Renault.

INSIDE A CAR ENGINE

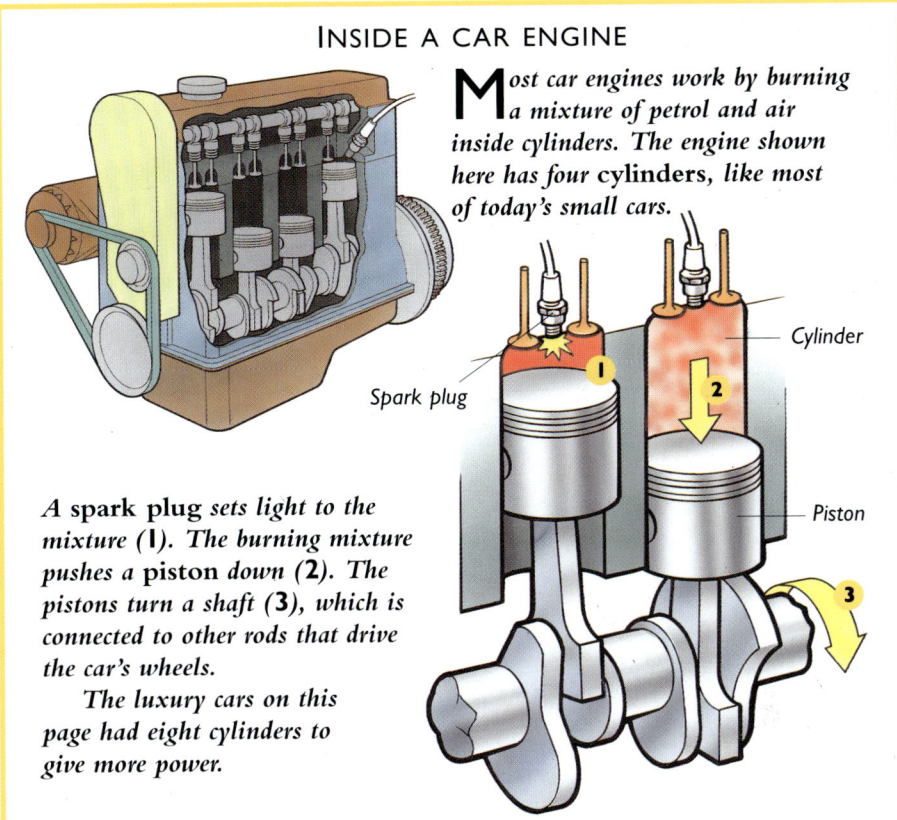

Most car engines work by burning a mixture of petrol and air inside cylinders. The engine shown here has four cylinders, like most of today's small cars.

Spark plug

Cylinder

Piston

A spark plug sets light to the mixture (1). The burning mixture pushes a piston down (2). The pistons turn a shaft (3), which is connected to other rods that drive the car's wheels.

The luxury cars on this page had eight cylinders to give more power.

▲ The dashboard and controls of this 1935 Mercedes were designed to look stylish as well as practical. The polished wood and shiny chrome gave an expensive feel. This Mercedes was made for export to Britain and has the steering wheel on the right. Cars made for Europe and the United States have the steering wheel on the left, making it easier to drive on the right-hand side of the road.

The large dial on the right is the speedometer, which shows how fast the car is travelling.

◄ The 1935 Auburn Speedster was one of the most stylish American sports cars ever built. Perhaps its owner was just about to take off in the waiting flying boat, a plane that could land on water. The Speedster was the ideal car for Hollywood film stars. It had a specially shaped locker for golf clubs, as well as a fitted radio, which was rare at the time.

The lettering on the bonnet reads 'SUPER-CHARGED'. This meant that the engine was boosted by a device called a supercharger to give it more power.

17

More cars for the people

In the 1930s a German company created a 'people's car' that has lasted right up to today. It was not a luxurious car, and some people considered it to be almost ugly. The car was nicknamed the Beetle because of its shape, and over 50 years it went on to become the best-selling car of all time.

The Volkswagen Beetle had its engine at the back and the luggage space, or boot, at the front. The engine was air-cooled by a fan, rather than water-cooled by a radiator. The basic shape of the car has stayed the same throughout its long life, with just small changes to the windows and lights.

Volkswagen and Porsche

In the early 1930s the German dictator, Adolf Hitler, decided that Germany needed a car that every worker could afford. In 1934 the first Volkswagen – German for 'people's car' – was designed by Ferdinand Porsche, who later became famous for his sports cars. In the mid-1930s, 1 in every 49 Germans owned a car, compared with 1 in 21 Britons and 1 in 5 Americans, so Germany had some catching-up to do. The idea was that workers could collect savings stamps to help buy a car. But in 1939 the Second World War broke out, and the Volkswagen factory was used to make military vehicles.

World bestseller

By the end of the war, in 1945, the Volkswagen factory had been badly damaged. The Americans and British saw little future for it, but in its first year the rebuilt factory produced almost 1800 Beetles. After that, the production figure just kept going up year after year. By 1965 the figure was over a million, and this had dropped only slightly by 1974, when the last Beetles were made in Germany. Altogether more than 21 million Beetles have been made, and they are still being produced in Mexico and Brazil. The German factory at Wolfsburg went over to producing the Golf and other VW models.

City cars

Although it also performed well on fast roads, the Beetle was considered to be a good car for town driving. Other European countries were also developing small cars that were cheap and easy to drive in the growing city traffic. Fiat launched their Topolino (or 'Little Mouse') in Italy in 1936. Britain's answer came in 1959, with the Mini, which packed everything a city car needed into a very small space. You can still buy this famous little car today.

HOW GEARS WORK

The gearwheels in a gearbox (below) change the speed of the car's driving wheels. The **input shaft** is turned by the engine. The **output shaft** turns the **drive shaft** that turns the car's wheels.

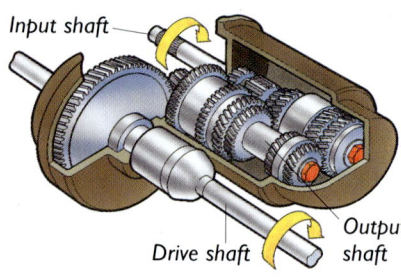

Input shaft

Drive shaft

Output shaft

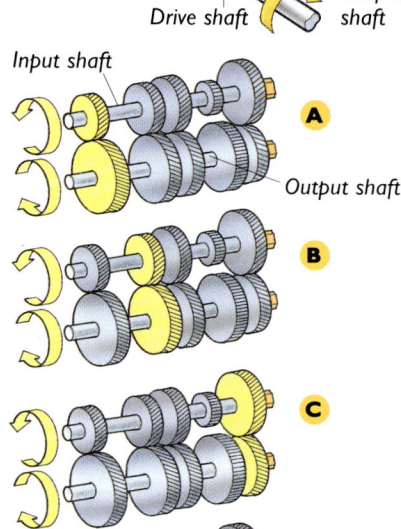

Input shaft

Output shaft

A

B

C

D

In first or bottom gear (**A**), a small gearwheel on the input shaft turns a large gearwheel on the output shaft. This turns the car's wheels slowly but with great power, which is good for starting off.

In second gear (**B**) the output shaft turns more quickly but with less power.

In fourth or top gear (**C**), the two gearwheels are the same size and so turn at the same speed. The car goes at its fastest.

The reverse gear (**D**) has a third gearwheel to turn the output shaft the other way.

▶ In the 1960s the Mini was a very fashionable car. This special model was launched in 1988, almost 30 years after the first Minis were made.

This small car was designed to save space. The engine was mounted sideways and drove the front wheels directly beneath it. The wheels were smaller than usual, too. This layout gave enough room for four adults to travel in the car, even though it was only 2.5 metres long. Minis are still produced today.

◀ Early motorists gave hand signals to show other road-users what they intended to do.

Then semaphore indicators, like the one shown above, were introduced. The indicator swung out and lit up to point in the direction the car was going to turn. In the 1950s these were replaced by flashing indicators.

▶ In the 1950s and 1960s many American cars were large, powerful and flashy, like this pink model parked by a hotel in Miami, Florida. Car companies such as Cadillac introduced bigger, curved **windscreens**, which increased visibility and added to safety, and fins at the back, which were just for show.

These cars were so big and heavy that they had to have **power-assisted steering** and brakes. These developments were later used in smaller cars.

21

▲ The Fiat Topolino was the smallest mass-produced car in the world when it came out in 1936. It was designed to carry two people and a small amount of luggage. It had a top speed of 85 kilometres per hour, and was very popular in the towns and cities of Italy.

▲ As the number of cars grew over the years, so too did the number of roads on which they could travel. In the United States, roads connected to form fast links between the different states. Today there is a network of numbered interstate highways across the whole country, shown on the map above.

The United States has more roads than any other country — over 6.2 million kilometres. The roads are needed, since there are far more cars there than anywhere else too — 143 million of them!

Supercars

Throughout the history of motoring, some drivers have been more interested in speed and style than in simply travelling from one place to another. The sport of motor racing is over 100 years old, and many of today's motorists dream of driving one of the world's supercars.

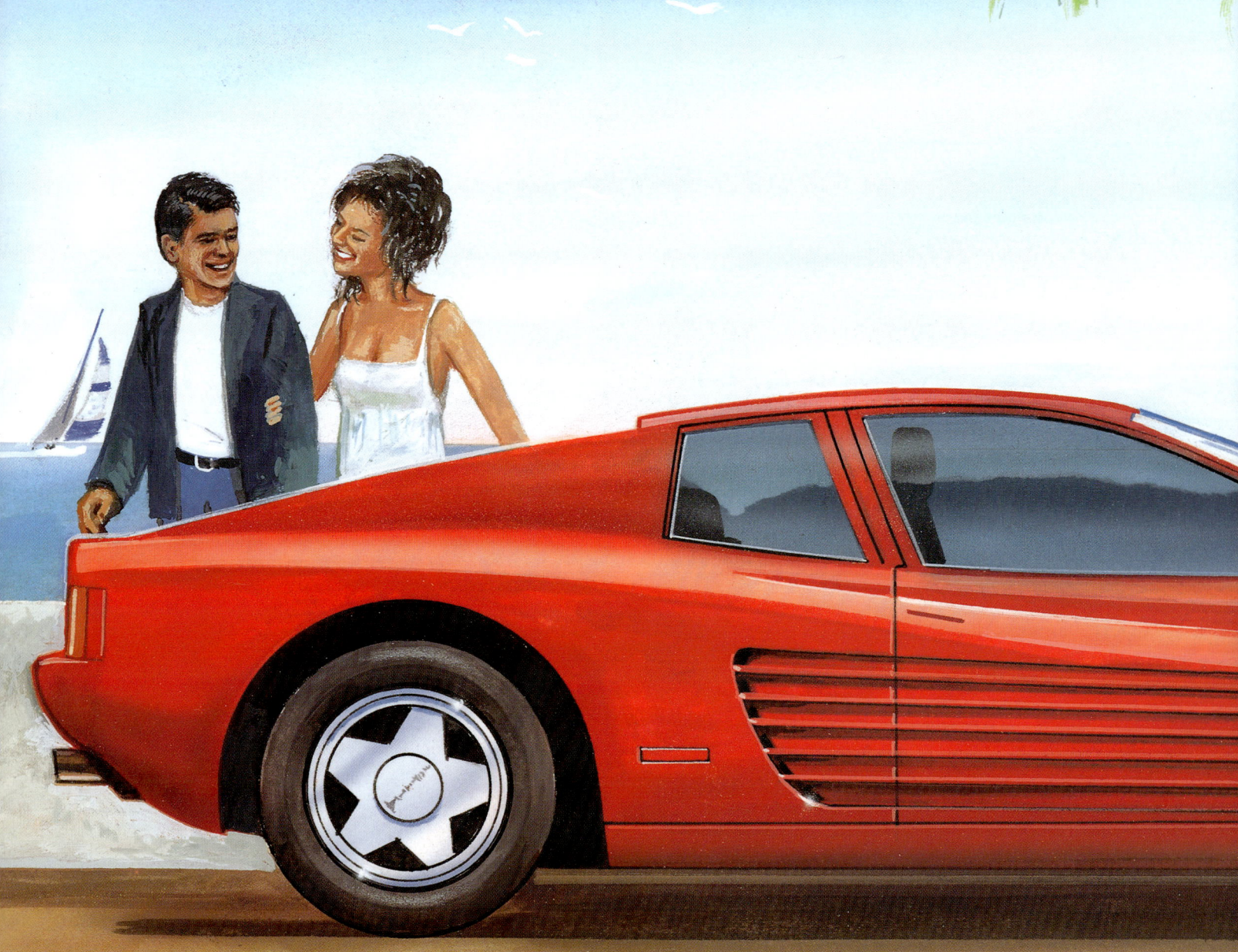

The Ferrari Testarossa (Italian for 'red head') was launched at the Paris Motor Show in 1984. It has a top speed of 290 kilometres per hour, well over twice as fast as most of the world's speed limits. The fins along the side of the car cover **air intakes** that help cool the huge engine behind the two seats.

Motor racing

The first motor race took place in France in 1894. It was run from Paris to Rouen and was won by Count de Dion driving his own steam car at an average speed of 18 kilometres per hour. The first **Grand Prix** race, also held in France, was won by a Renault car at the much higher speed of 101 kilometres per hour. By the 1920s many sports cars could top 160 kilometres per hour, and car companies realized that success in road races and on the track helped sell their cars to the general public. Alfa Romeo, Bugatti, Bentley and Chevrolet cars all earned great racing reputations and were bought by motoring enthusiasts.

High-performance cars

Technical improvements were made to cars so that they would win races. These improvements were often passed on to everyday road cars, though they usually improved speed and performance rather than economy or safety. Ferrari is just one car company that makes racing cars for the track and sports cars for the road. Enzo Ferrari, who founded the company in 1929, was himself a racing driver with another Italian firm, Alfa Romeo. He used all the knowledge he gained as a driver to make the most stylish sports cars. The Testarossa was one in a long line of these.

Sheer speed

Most countries have an overall speed limit of about 110 kilometres per hour, even on the fastest roads. You might think this makes cars capable of any higher speed unnecessary, but today the smallest, most ordinary car can go faster than that. Some supercars can go three times faster! In 1992 a Jaguar travelled at 349 kilometres per hour on a test track. And the McLaren F1 is a road version of the car that won the Le Mans 24-hour race in 1995. Its top speed is 372 kilometres per hour!

▲ Many sports car manufacturers build racing cars too. Ferrari's famous cars have been running in Grand Prix races since 1948. The red Ferraris are cheered on by Italian supporters all over the world, even though they are often driven by non-Italians.

Two famous racing drivers are pictured here: Niki Lauda of Austria, in the 1975 Ferrari 312T(top), which won the manufacturer's world championship that year, and Michael Schumacher of Germany, in the 1996 Ferrari F310 (above), which came second in the world championship.

24

THE WORLD'S FASTEST GARAGE

*R*acing slicks wear out very quickly and have to be changed in Grand Prix races. The cars go into the pits and fill up with petrol at the same time. This is all done very quickly, so that the car loses as little time in the race as possible, and it takes a crew of about 20 people. If all goes well, the wheel-changing and refuelling takes less than ten seconds!

There is a team of three for each wheel: a mechanic to take off and put on the wheel nuts, another to take the old wheel off, and a third to put a new wheel on. The picture shows what all the mechanics do.

1 **jacks up** the back end of the car.
2 jacks up the front end.
3 takes off and puts on the wheel nuts.
4 takes the old wheel off.
5 puts the new wheel on.
6 puts petrol in.
7 holds the fuel hose.

8 stands ready for an emergency, such as a fire.
9 cuts the flow of fuel in an emergency.
10 cleans the driver's helmet visor.
11 shows a board to tell the driver when to go.

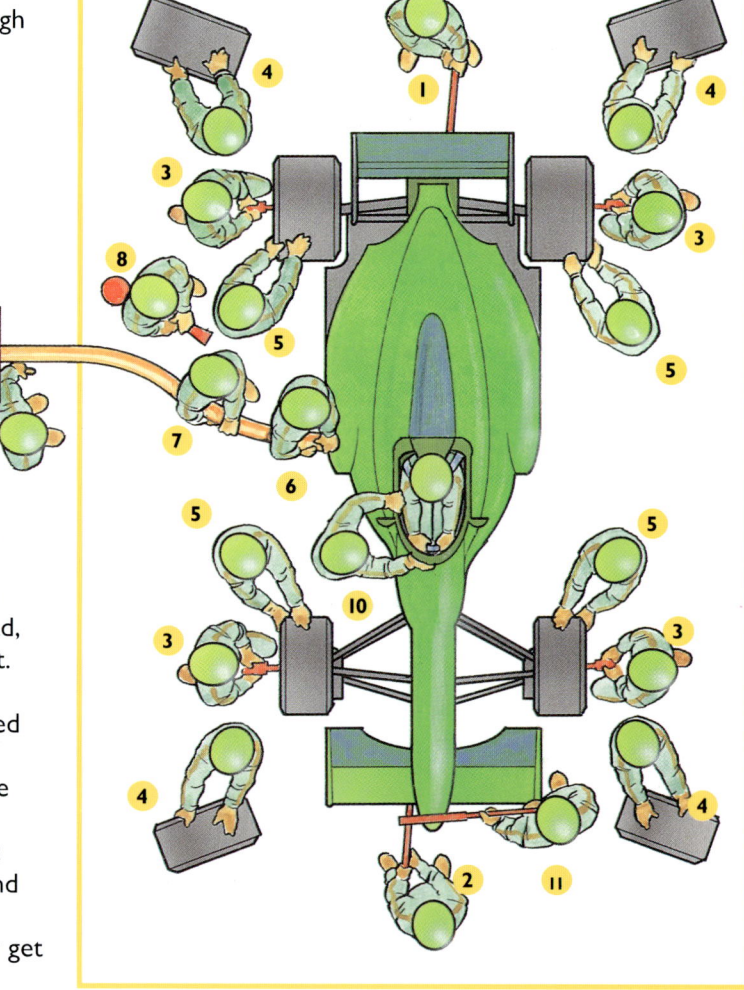

◄ Most car tyres have a tread – a pattern of grooves that helps the tyre grip the road, especially in the wet. Racing cars use smooth tyres, called **slicks**, when the track is dry. These tyres put more rubber in contact with the track, and they grip even better when they get warm and sticky.

HOW BRAKES WORK

Modern cars use a system of disc brakes. Some cars have **drum brakes** on the rear wheels. The discs and drums are inside the wheels of the car.

When a driver presses the brake pedal, special fluid is pumped to the brakes. The brake fluid operates pads that press against a disc inside the wheel. This slows down the disc and the wheel.

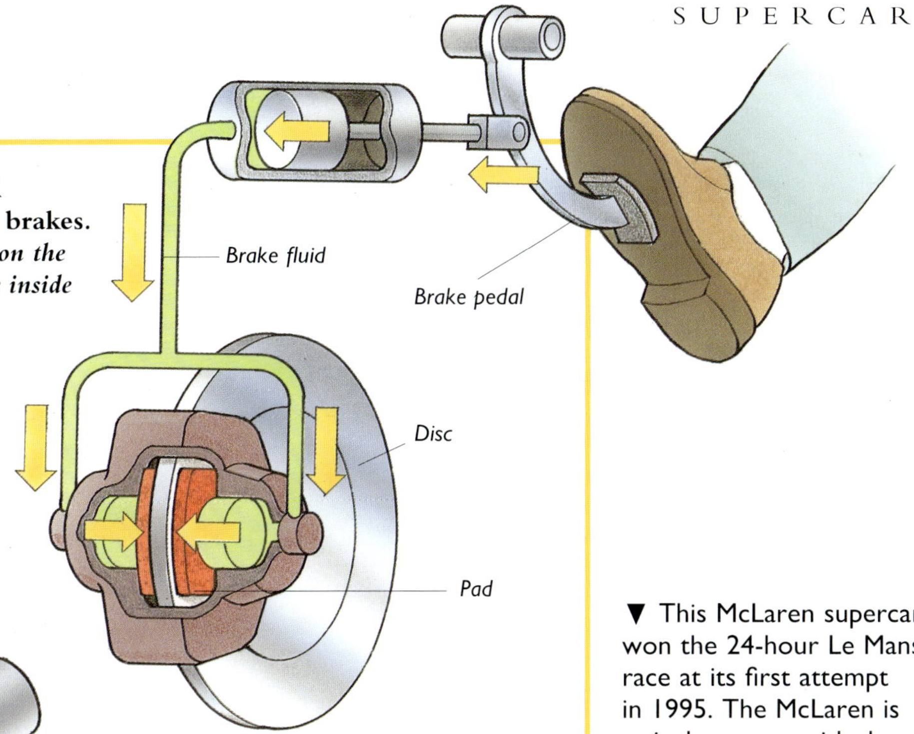

Brake fluid

Brake pedal

Disc

Pad

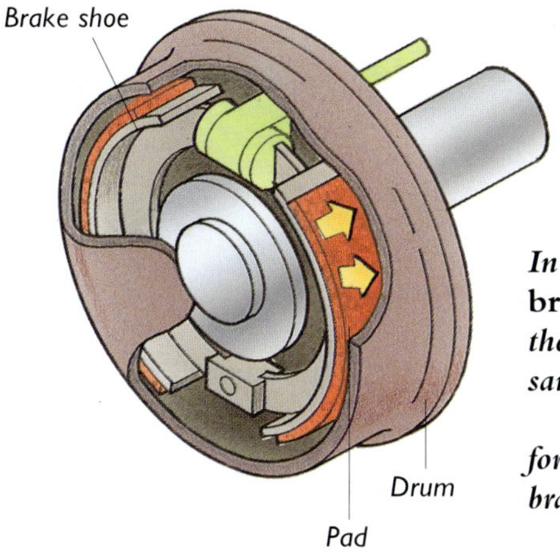

Brake shoe

Drum

Pad

In drum brakes, the brake pads are on curved **brake shoes**, which press against the inside of the drum. The drum is slowed down in the same way as a disc.

Both systems need only a small pushing force on the brake pedal to apply a very great braking force to the wheels.

▼ This McLaren supercar won the 24-hour Le Mans race at its first attempt in 1995. The McLaren is a single-seater, with the driving position in the centre of the car.

Wealthy supercar enthusiasts can buy their own road-going version, which has two extra seats for passengers. It is the fastest and probably the most expensive car that ordinary drivers can buy.

25

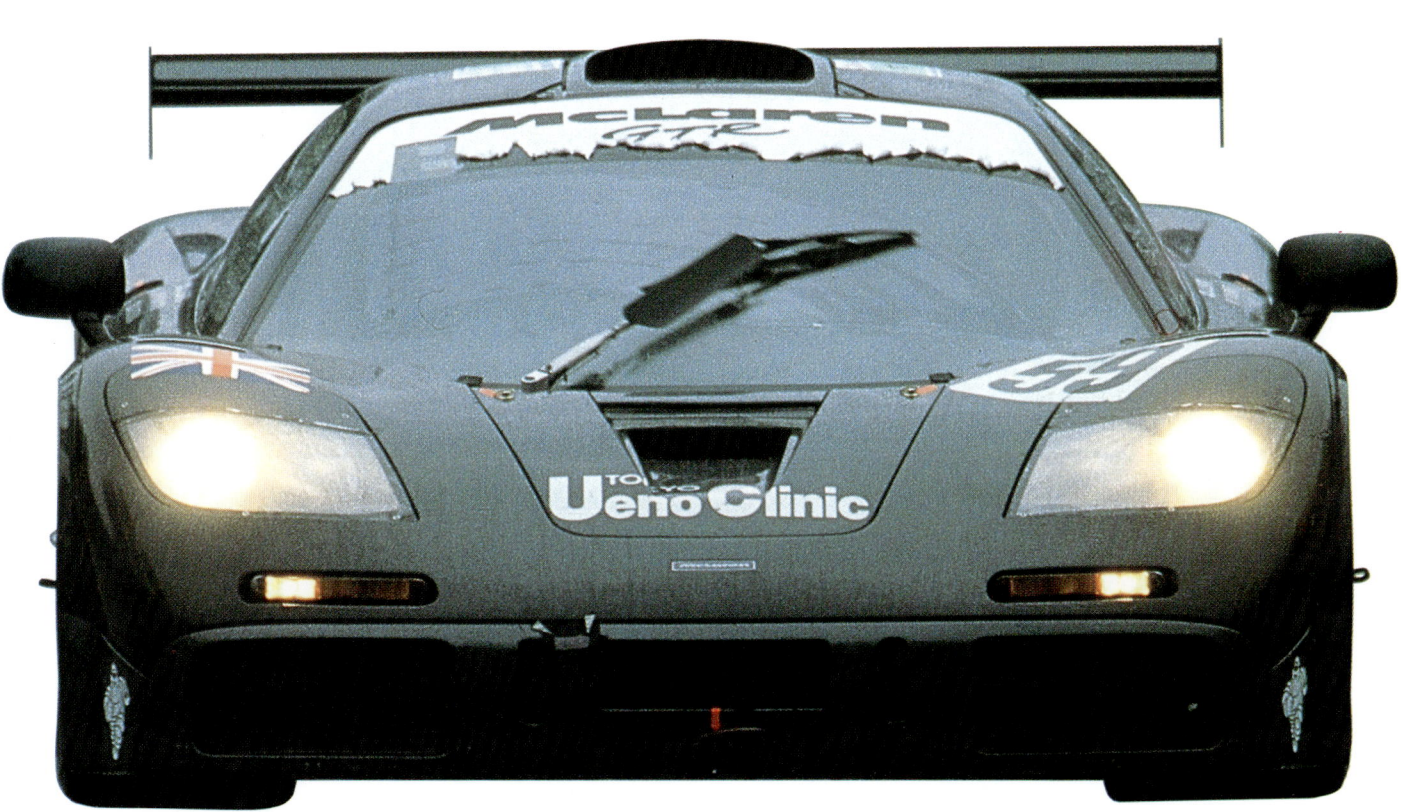

Modern technology

Compared with the early days of motoring a century ago, travelling by car today is smooth and enjoyable. As you drive along a well-surfaced road, you sit in a comfortable seat, with the heater on in winter, perhaps listening to the in-car stereo.

The Toyota Previa is one of several multi-seater cars launched in the 1990s. They are often called multi-purpose vehicles, people-movers or space-wagons. This car has enough room for the driver and seven passengers, but it is only 25 centimetres longer than the two-seater Ferrari Testarossa. The engine is mounted under the floor.

New developments

Many recent car developments have come about because we have realized that exhaust fumes harm people and the environment. Now all new cars run on **unleaded petrol** and have **catalytic converters**, which stop some of the fumes. Modern cars are much safer than ever before, with better brakes and features such as **airbags**, which inflate inside the car if it is in an accident. But still many journeys are made by people on their own in the car, which is a waste of energy and causes traffic jams. Space-wagons help with this problem, allowing families and friends to travel together.

An unequal world

Japanese, American and German companies produce most cars in the world. In the United States, there is one automobile for every two people in the country. In North America, Europe, Japan and other rich parts of the world, many people think of travelling by car as an absolute necessity. As other forms of transport, such as railways, have been cut back, people have come to rely totally on their cars. But in many other, poorer countries, people still think of a car as a luxury, as it once was everywhere.

Into the future

In the twenty-first century car manufacturers and motorists will be looking for more and more ways to save energy. There were electric cars many years ago, and now they are being developed again as an alternative to cars using petrol. Perhaps ways will be found to encourage people to keep their cars longer, instead of buying a new one. Old parts are already being recycled. The first 100 years of motoring have been an exciting period of travel, and perhaps cars will change just as much again in the next century.

CRASH TESTING

Safety is very important to today's motorists, and manufacturers test the safety features of their cars using dummies as drivers and passengers. Cars are purposely crashed head–on into walls to test the crumple zone at the front. This part of the car crumples easily, while the rigid passenger compartment stays intact.

In the car on the left, the dummy driver is protected by the front crumple zone, a seat belt and an airbag. The pictures below show how the airbag system works.

1 The airbag is stored in the middle of the steering wheel. If the car crashes, an automatic sensor pushes the air bag out in milliseconds. Then chemicals start to fill the bag with gas.

2 As the driver is thrown forward, the bag completely fills with air. It forms a soft pillow for the driver's chest and head, stopping her from hitting the steering wheel and protecting her from injury.

3 The driver's seat belt also helps to stop her going forward. The airbag will not come out if there is only a gentle front-on crash or if the car is hit from behind or from the side.

▶ A Jeep Grand Cherokee climbs a bumpy mountain track. This is a **four-wheel drive** vehicle, which means that all four wheels are driven by the engine. This gives extra grip, especially on rough, hilly ground. In most cars, the engine drives just two wheels – either the front or the rear pair. Four-wheel drive cars are popular on good roads and in towns, too.

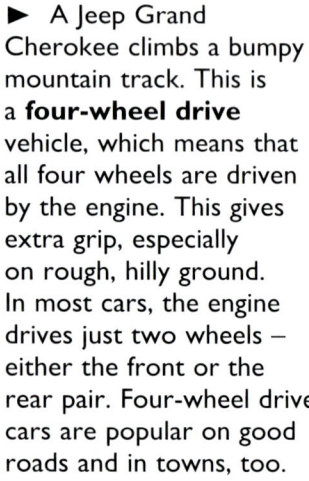

◀ Car factories still use the assembly-line system introduced by Henry Ford over 80 years ago. But today, many of the workers have been replaced by computerized robots. Body shells move between rows of robots, which weld the different parts together. The robots are expensive to install, but they can help produce many identical cars very quickly.

▼ The **aerodynamics** of a car are very important. The easier it can slip through the air, the faster the car can go and the less petrol it uses. Full-scale models are put in wind tunnels to test their aerodynamics, and this can also be simulated by a powerful computer, as shown here. These tests help designers develop an efficient shape for new models.

29

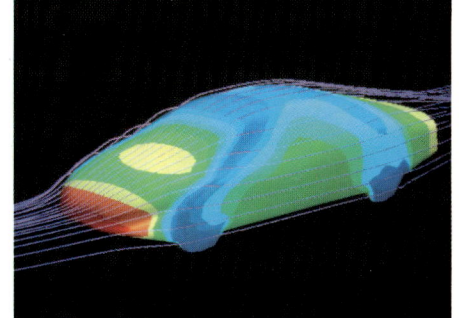

▶ Instead of filling up at a petrol station, this electric car has its batteries re-charged.

Petrol-driven cars cause many problems. The oil from which petrol comes will one day be in very short supply, and the exhaust fumes from petrol engines cause pollution. Electric cars are one alternative being investigated, and some electric models are already available.

Glossary

aerodynamics The streamlined features of a car that allow it to slip through the air faster.

airbag A large plastic bag which inflates inside the car if it is in an accident, to protect the driver.

air intake Openings on the sides of the car to let air in to cool a car's engine.

brake shoe A curved piece of metal in a drum brake, which presses a pad against the drum to slow the car down.

catalytic converter A metal box in a car's exhaust system that cuts down some of the poisonous gases that come from the engine.

chassis The frame and wheels of a car, to which the body is attached.

coachwork The body of a car.

crank handle A handle which early motorists had to turn to start a car's engine.

30

cylinder A chamber in an engine, in which fuel burns.

dashboard The panel of dials and switches in front of a car's driver.

disc brake A brake that slows the car down by pressing pads against a disc inside the wheel.

drive shaft The rod that is turned by the output shaft and turns a car's wheels.

drum brake A brake that slows the car down by pressing pads against a drum inside the wheel.

exhaust fumes Gases given off by a car engine as it works.

four-wheel drive A system in which all four of a car's wheels are driven by the engine.

gear A gearwheel or a set of gearwheels that changes the speed of the car's driving wheels.

gearbox The metal casing that contains a car's gearwheels.

gearwheel A toothed wheel that fits into another toothed wheel and turns it.

Grand Prix An important motor race. The words are French for 'great prize'.

input shaft The rod that is turned by a car's engine and goes into the gearbox.

internal combustion engine A normal car engine, which works by burning fuel inside cylinders.

jack up To lift up with a lever called a jack.

output shaft The rod that is turned by a car's gearwheels.

patent A certificate that allows an inventor to sell his invention and prevents his idea from being copied by anyone else.

pedestrian zone An area where there are no cars and people are allowed to travel only on foot.

petrol A liquid made from oil that is stored in a car's fuel tank and burned in the engine to make it work.

piston A part that slides to and fro in an engine's cylinder and turns the input shaft.

pollution Damage caused by poisonous and harmful substances.

power-assisted steering A system in which the power of a car's engine is used to make the steering wheel easier to turn.

radiator A system of tubes containing water that is used to cool a car's engine.

slick A smooth racing tyre without a tread.

spark plug A device that makes an electric spark to set light to fuel in an engine.

throttle A control that lets more fuel into the engine to make the car go faster.

unleaded petrol Petrol that does not contain lead and so causes less pollution.

windscreen The large front window of a car.

31

Index